Frank, Sarah
    Filipinos in America

FILIPINOS IN AMERICA

web enhanced at www.inamericabooks.com

SARAH FRANK

LERNER PUBLICATIONS COMPANY // MINNEAPOLIS

Current information and statistics quickly become out of date. That's why we developed **www.inamericabooks.com**, a companion website to the **In America** series. The site offers lots of additional information—downloadable photos and maps and up-to-date facts through links to additional websites. Each link has been carefully selected by researchers at Lerner Publishing Group and is regularly reviewed and updated. However, Lerner Publishing Group is not responsible for the accuracy or suitability of material on websites that are not maintained directly by us. It is recommended that students using the Internet be supervised by a parent, a librarian, a teacher, or another adult.

Copyright © 2006 by Lerner Publications Company

All rights reserved. International copyright secured. No part of this book may be reproduced, stored in a retrieval system, or transmitted in any form or by any means—electronic, mechanical, photocopying, recording, or otherwise—without the prior written permission of Lerner Publications Company, except for the inclusion of brief quotations in an acknowledged review.

Lerner Publications Company
A division of Lerner Publishing Group
241 First Avenue North
Minneapolis, MN 55401 U.S.A.

Website address: www.lernerbooks.com

Library of Congress Cataloging-in-Publication Data
Frank, Sarah, 1978–
    Filipinos in America / by Sarah Frank.
      p.   cm. — (In America)
    Includes bibliographical references and index.
    ISBN-13: 978-0-8225-4873-7 (lib. bdg. : alk. paper)
    ISBN-10: 0-8225-4873-9 (lib. bdg. : alk. paper)
    1. Filipino Americans–Juvenile literature. 2. Filipino Americans–History–Juvenile Literature.
3. Immigrants–United States–History–Juvenile literature. I. Title. II. Series: In America (Minneapolis, Minn.)
    E184.F4F73 2006
    973′.049921–dc22   2004028543

Manufactured in the United States of America
1 2 3 4 5 6 – JR – 11 10 09 08 07 06

CONTENTS

INTRODUCTION

In America, a walk down a city street can seem like a walk through many lands. Grocery stores sell international foods. Shops offer products from around the world. People strolling past may speak foreign languages. This unique blend of cultures is the result of America's history as a nation of immigrants.

Native peoples have lived in North America for centuries. The next settlers were the Vikings. In about A.D. 1000, they sailed from Scandinavia to lands that would become Canada, Greenland, and Iceland. In 1492 the Italian navigator Christopher Columbus landed in the Americas, and more European explorers arrived during the 1500s. In the 1600s, British settlers formed colonies that, after the Revolutionary War (1775–1783), would become the United States. And in the mid-1800s, a great wave of immigration brought millions of new arrivals to the young country.

Immigrants have many different reasons for leaving home. They may leave to escape poverty, war, or harsh governments. They may want better living conditions for themselves and their children. Throughout its history, America has been known as a nation that offers many opportunities. For this reason, many immigrants come to America.

Moving to a new country is not easy. It can mean making a long, difficult journey. It means leaving home and starting over in an unfamiliar place. But it also means using skill, talent, and determination to build a new life. The In America series tells the story of immigration to the United States and the search for fresh beginnings in a new country—in America.

FILIPINOS IN AMERICA

The first confirmed Filipino immigrants arrived in New Orleans in 1763. They came aboard galleons, or Spanish sailing ships, that traveled between the Philippines and Mexico. The Spanish knew that Filipino sailors were excellent seamen. They often enlisted Filipinos for service on the galleons.

The first major wave of Filipino immigrants to the United States did not arrive until the early to mid 1900s. They settled in Hawaii, where plantation owners hired them to work in the sugar and pineapple industries. They also came to California, Alaska, and the Pacific Northwest, where they worked on farms and in lumberyards and canneries. Conditions in the United States were difficult for the first wave of immigrants. Filipinos performed hard labor and did not make enough money to provide for themselves. Worse than the low pay was the discrimination they faced. In California people looked down on Filipinos. "Positively No Filipinos Allowed" signs were common.

With the second and third waves of Filipino immigration, conditions in the United States began to improve. Immigrants arriving in the second wave—between 1950 and 1960—found jobs as clerks, accountants, and in other fields originally closed to them. When the third wave arrived between 1961 and 1985, Filipinos were working in the arts, law, medicine, and many other industries.

By the twenty-first century, the United States was home to 2.4 million people with Filipino ancestry. Filipinos continue to be a growing influence in America—in business, arts, politics, and culture.

1 THE HISTORY OF THE PHILIPPINES

The Philippines is a one-thousand-mile-long archipelago, or group of islands, in the western Pacific Ocean. It is made up of more than 7,100 islands, which stretch between Taiwan in the north and Indonesia in the south. The climate in the Philippines is very hot, and the land is covered with lush vegetation. The nation's capital is Manila, which is located on the island of Luzon.

PRE-HISPANIC TIMES

People may have first lived in the Philippines half a million years ago. Stone tools and signs of cooking fires are evidence of life from that time. During the last Ice Age, hunters probably came to the Philippines from China and the Malayan archipelago. They crossed over natural land bridges that

The Negritos typically stand less than five feet tall. They are traditionally hunters and gatherers, using tools such as bows and arrows (above) for the hunt.

existed because the waters around the islands were much lower then.

Other migrants used the land bridges too. About twenty-five thousand to thirty thousand years ago, a group of people reached the Philippines from the south. The new arrivals were good hunters who used arrows and darts. They were the ancestors of the Negritos, people who live in rain forests in northern Luzon. Later migrants came from Borneo twelve thousand to fifteen thousand years ago. These people knew how to use blowguns and to grow crops in forest clearings. They built houses from tree branches and the large banana leaves that grow in the Philippines.

When the Ice Age ended about ten thousand years ago, rising waters covered the land bridges that connected the Philippines to the rest of Asia. The first migrants to travel to the islands by sea were Indonesians. They arrived five thousand to six thousand years ago. Using axes, chisels, and other tools made of stone, these people hunted, fished, trapped, and farmed. Large groups of immigrants also came from what are now southern China and Vietnam.

The most important of the newcomers to the Philippines were the Malays. The Malays were from the Malayan archipelago. They began arriving in about 1500 B.C. Either this group or a later wave of Malays created the fantastic rice terraces along the mountains in Luzon.

THE RICE TERRACES OF LUZON

Rice terraces are common in Asia, but the most remarkable are in the Philippines. Spanning 49,400 acres along the mountains of northern Luzon, the terraces *(right)* rise into the sky like enormous steps. The terraces stay moist with the help of a large system of bamboo tubes. Water from natural waterfalls flows through the tubes and travels to the terraces. In order to create the beautiful landscape, Malays carved into rugged terrain using nothing more than ancient tools. The elaborate beauty of the terraces shows how talented and resourceful their creators were.

Iron Age Malays from the island of Borneo came to the Philippines between 300 and 200 B.C. They introduced iron, glass, and the art of weaving. They also brought a written language. Malay migrants would continue to arrive in the Philippines up to the fifteenth century A.D.

In the seventh century, a powerful empire called Sri Vijaya arose in the Malayan archipelago. This empire controlled trade in Southeast Asia for about five hundred years. Sri Vijaya gave its name to the central Philippine island group called the Visayas.

FIND LINKS TO LEARN MORE ABOUT THE HISTORY OF THE PHILIPPINES AT WWW.INAMERICABOOKS.COM.

The empire of Sri Vijaya gave way to an empire called Majapahit. Majapahit governors in the Philippines were called sealords. Sealords used ships and troops to keep order. They practiced the Hindu religion. To help keep peace in the empire, however, the sealords did not try to change the Filipinos' religious beliefs. Filipinos continued their practice of worshipping gods of nature. Nevertheless, the Majapahit Hindu culture did influence the people of the Philippines.

During the first part of the Majapahit Empire or perhaps even earlier, Chinese traders introduced their culture to the Philippines. The Filipinos treasured Chinese silk, porcelains, and other Chinese goods. They traded pearls, shells, mats, and wax for these items. Filipinos respected the Chinese culture. For a short time, the Filipinos even allowed the Chinese to control parts of their islands. Eventually, however, traders from the Arabian peninsula forced the Chinese out.

Abu Ali was perhaps the first Arab trader to visit the Philippines. He arrived in 977. By the fourteenth century, the Philippine economy benefited from being a crossroads between Arab and Chinese trade. In addition to bringing money and goods into the archipelago, the Arabs spread the Muslim religion, Islam. In about 1380, the Arabian scholar Mudum (or Mahdum) arrived in the southern islands of the Sulu group. He began teaching Filipinos about the Muslim faith. A decade later, much of Sulu was practicing Islam.

MAGELLAN'S VOYAGE

On March 16, 1521, three Spanish galleons sailed toward what looked like the tip of a large island in the western Pacific. The three ships, commanded by Portuguese–born captain Ferdinand Magellan, had reached the southern end of the island of Samar. Magellan named the island Saint Lazarus. It was the official European discovery of the archipelago later called the Philippines.

Not often mentioned in history books, however, is a trip Magellan had made nine years earlier. In 1512 Magellan set sail on a secret voyage from Malacca in Malaysia. It was then that he first discovered the Philippines. He may have visited the Chinese settlement of Paria on Luzon and cruised around the archipelago.

Captain Ferdinand Magellan was a bold Portuguese explorer who captained the voyage that eventually circumnavigated the world. Though Magellan did not live to see the completion of this landmark journey, the voyage offered positive proof that the world was indeed round.

Magellan lands in the Philippines in 1521. Magellan's crew formed close relationships with the islanders and took great pride in converting many islanders to their religion, Christianity.

Magellan was amazed at the gold mines and precious pearls of Luzon. He made up his mind to return.

Magellan's second expedition took him south from Spain, through the straits at the tip of South America (now named after Magellan), and across the wide Pacific. After reaching Guam on March 6, 1521, Magellan continued his journey and landed on a small, uninhabited island in the Philippine archipelago. There his crew feasted on coconuts, papayas, mangos, and other delicious fruits unknown to the Europeans.

Magellan and his crew sailed on. Eventually they reached the inhabited island of Limasawa. Magellan felt sure he was in the Spice Islands. He did not realize he had set foot in the Philippines for the second time. On a hill above Limasawa, Magellan claimed the entire archipelago for the Spanish king, Charles I. He named it the Islands of Saint Lazarus.

While on Limasawa, Magellan learned that Cebu was the largest and richest island in the Philippines. He set out for Cebu and reached it on April 7, 1521. Humabon, the ruler of the island, was unhappy to see the foreign invader at first. Eventually, however, Magellan's servant, Enrique (who spoke the same language as Humabon), convinced Humabon to befriend the Europeans. Humabon then recognized Spain as the ruler of his lands. He even agreed to accept the religion of Christianity.

Not all Filipinos were as willing as Humabon to give up their religion and customs. Magellan got word that Lapu-Lapu, the chief of the neighboring small island of Mactan, refused to accept Spanish rule. Magellan decided to punish Lapu-Lapu by leading an expedition to Mactan. This was a deadly mistake.

The overconfident Magellan relied upon only 50 untrained volunteers for his fighting force. The fighters wore heavy armor that made it difficult for them to move on the muddy beach of Mactan.

Lapu-Lapu's army of 1,500 warriors easily beat Magellan's men. Magellan, who almost became the first person to sail around the world, died on April 27, 1521, fighting on the Philippine island of Mactan. Chief Lapu-Lapu became a hero—the first Filipino to successfully drive out a foreign invader. A statue of him now stands on Mactan.

The few survivors of Magellan's army made it back to Cebu. One of Magellan's ships continued the

This statue of Chief Lapu-Lapu stands on Mactan commemorating the brave stand he made against Magellan's expedition in 1521.

voyage, crossing the Indian Ocean and sailing around the southern tip of Africa. On September 6, 1522, the ship reached Seville, Spain, the starting point of Magellan's expedition three years earlier. Thus the first voyage around the world was completed.

FOUR CENTURIES UNDER SPAIN

After Magellan's expedition, the Spanish repeatedly crossed the Pacific. They were still searching for the spices of the East. An explorer named Ruy Lopez de Villalobos made one of these voyages. In February 1543, Villalobos reached the southeastern part of the island of Mindanao. He renamed some of the archipelago's islands the Felipinas, after the Spanish prince who later became King Philip II. Villalobos planned to establish a settlement in the Philippines, but his expedition failed. He did not have enough supplies, and the Filipinos he met on his trip were not welcoming to the foreign invader.

Not until 1565 did the Spanish set up a permanent settlement in the archipelago. Miguel López de Legaspi, who worked for the Spanish government in Mexico City, led the important expedition. The explorers sailed from Mexico on four ships carrying four hundred men, as well as four missionaries who came to convert the Filipinos to the Christian religion. San Miguel (later named Cebu) was the first Spanish colony Legaspi established in the Philippines.

The Spanish expedition faced famine and fierce fighting by Filipino leaders who refused to accept Spanish control. Nevertheless, Legaspi succeeded in exploring a large part of the archipelago. By 1571 Legaspi established Manila as the capital of the Spanish colony. The spread of Islam north toward Luzon was stopped, but the Muslims were never conquered. Many mountain people also resisted change.

The Spanish united the islands of the Philippines into a single country with a new capital. They introduced schools and a common language. But the Spanish were not good leaders. Spain's conquest of the Philippines benefited the mother country much more than it did the colony.

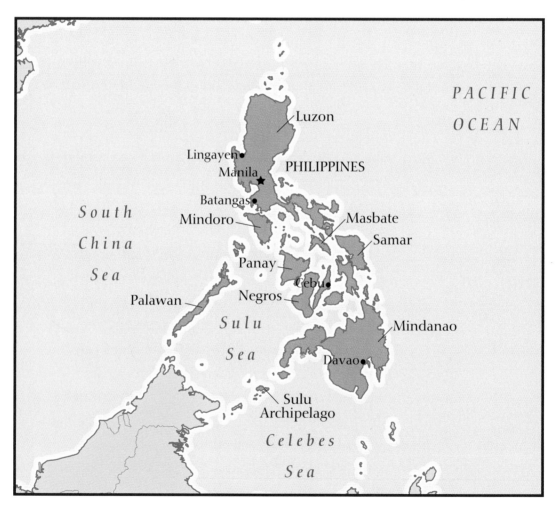

Download this map of the Philippines and other maps at www.inamericabooks.com.

A MELTING POT

The modern Philippines is a reflection of the country's complex history. It is a melting pot made up of many different cultures and religions. While the Philippines is mostly English speaking, Filipinos speak more than eighty different languages and dialects, including their native language of Tagalog. Even though many people and places have Spanish names, only a small number of Filipinos speak Spanish. That is because Spanish was exclusively the language of the upper classes during the period when Spain controlled the islands. Due to more than four hundred years of rule by Catholic Spain, the Philippine population is about 85 percent Roman Catholic. About 5 percent of Filipinos are Muslims, or followers of Islam, a result of contact with Arab and other Muslim traders who often traveled to the islands. There are many Muslim mosques, or temples, on the big southern island of Mindanao. The remaining 10 percent of the Philippine population are Buddhists or members of small Christian churches.

Spanish power in the colony was largely in the hands of missionaries. The missionaries owned plantations and forced Filipinos to work on them. Missionaries controlled the schools and taught mainly religious subjects. Few of the Filipino people, however, learned to speak Spanish. It was easier for the missionaries to learn the Filipinos' languages than for them to teach Spanish to the Filipinos.

The colonial Spanish government in Manila was corrupt. The king and colonial governor's chosen men were in charge, and they exploited Filipinos in the country and the cities. They forced them to work for the Spanish rulers.

For the first two hundred years of Spanish rule, the Philippines relied mainly on the galleon trade for support. In this trading system, the Chinese came to Manila and sold silk, diamonds, and other goods to the Spanish for Mexican silver. The silver arrived on galleons from the main Spanish–Mexican port of Acapulco. The Chinese goods were in turn loaded onto the same galleons, which then returned to Acapulco. Because of the dominance of the galleon trade, Philippine agriculture and industry—as well as the welfare of the people—were neglected.

During the late eighteenth century, economic conditions started to improve. The Philippines grew and exported tobacco, abacá (also called Manila hemp and used to make rope), and sugarcane. Yet Filipinos still had no control of their government. During the first quarter of the nineteenth century, several revolts broke out. But the Filipinos had no strong leadership or common identity, so the revolts failed.

The Spanish Empire itself soon began to decline. It started to lose its American colonies, including Mexico in 1821. During the same period, Philippine trading increased. A Filipino newspaper began, and a private university opened in Manila in 1859. A small educated class of native Filipinos arose.

CHECK OUT WWW.INAMERICABOOKS.COM FOR LINKS TO MORE INFORMATION ABOUT THE DECLINE OF THE SPANISH EMPIRE IN THE PHILIPPINES.

THE FIRST FILIPINO IMMIGRANTS

The profitable shipping trade between the Philippines and Mexico during the first two hundred years of Spanish colonial rule was responsible for bringing the first Filipinos to what is now the United States. There was always a shortage of crew members aboard the sailing ships, especially because of the harsh treatment that the sailors received from the ships' captains. Many sailors jumped ship once they got to the shore of a new land. The Spanish captains knew that Filipino sailors were some of the best. They recruited them—sometimes by force—to work on their ships.

The first Filipino immigrants (who were called "a few Luzon Indians" by the Spanish) sailed on the *Nuestra Señora de Esperanza* (*Our Lady of Hope*). The ship was commanded by Pedro de Unamuno. On October 18, 1587, the ship entered Morro Bay, near San Luis Obispo, California. It sent a landing party to shore. The party included the "Luzon Indians," who served as scouts and carried swords as protection against the Native Americans.

The landing party took official possession of the area for Spain by putting up a cross made of branches. The group was attacked by Native Americans, however, and one of the Filipinos was killed. Heavy fog rolled in, and Unamuno and his crew gave up further exploration of that part of the California coast. The first Filipino immigrants to create a permanent settlement in the United States did not arrive until 1763.

SHE IS GETTING TOO FEEBLE TO HOLD THEM.

This American political cartoon shows the queen of Spain struggling to hold onto two boys, Cuba and the Philippine Islands, each one symbolizing a colony trying to gain independence.

THE PHILIPPINE REVOLUTION

Many educated Filipinos wanted to get rid of the corrupt Spanish government. José Rizal was one Filipino who spoke out against the foreign invaders. Rizal was a doctor of medicine, a poet, and a novelist. He wrote books about the problems he saw in his country. Rizal and his followers started the Filipino League. This group worked toward peaceful reform of the islands.

> *We want the happiness of the Philippines, but we want to obtain it through noble and just means, for right is on our side and therefore we ought not to do anything wrong. If I have to act villainously in order to make my country happy, I would refuse to do it because I am sure that what is built on sand sooner or later would tumble down.*
>
> —*José Rizal*

Unlike Rizal, some Filipinos did not think peaceful protest could make a difference. They formed a secret group that used violence against the government. In 1896 fighting began. Rizal was unfairly accused of starting the violence, and he was put to death.

Under the leadership of Emilio Aguinaldo, the rebels continued fighting. They finally forced the Spaniards to sign the pact of Biacna–Bato. In the pact, the Spanish government guaranteed reforms within three years, including full civil rights for Filipinos. But in 1898, the Spanish–American War broke out when the United States supported the independence movement of the Spanish colony of Cuba. The Philippines became involved when a U.S. squadron under Commodore George Dewey sailed to Manila from Hong Kong and destroyed the Spanish fleet in Manila Bay.

The United States promised Filipino independence if Aguinaldo and his followers would help the United States in the battles against the Spanish. The Filipinos did their part. They rejoiced when they defeated Spain in August 1898. The United States, however, did not keep its promise. The United States and Spain signed a document called the Treaty of Paris. This document gave independence to Cuba but

put the Philippines and other Spanish colonies in the hands of the United States.

Aguinaldo had already declared Filipino independence and felt betrayed. U.S. leaders claimed that the Philippines was not yet ready for independence. However, the military and commercial value of controlling an Asian country may have influenced the United States' decision to take over the Philippines.

Aguinaldo and his followers continued their struggle for independence, this time against the United States. The bloody conflict dragged on for three years until Aguinaldo was finally captured in

The May 1, 1898, battle in Manila Bay destroyed the entire Spanish fleet without the loss of American life or serious damage to any of Commodore Dewey's ships. The victory made Dewey a hero in the United States and made the United States a great power in the Pacific Ocean.

1901. Realizing the hopelessness of his position, he then pledged his loyalty to the United States.

Under the Stars and Stripes

Conditions were still unsettled in the Philippines. The United States sent soldiers to help keep the country secure and to serve as teachers in Filipino schools. It also set up a school to train Filipino teachers. In 1908 the government-supported University of the Philippines opened its doors in Manila.

Little by little, the Philippines gained its independence. The United States began placing Filipinos in government jobs and gradually loosened its control of the Filipino government. In 1916, for the

[In U.S.-run schools], . . . education became miseducation because it began to de-Filipinize the youth, taught them to regard American culture as superior to any other, and American society as the model . . . for Philippine society.

—Filipino historian Renato Constantino

A group of students learns English at a U.S-run school in the Philippines.

first time, Filipinos elected members to their Senate and House of Representatives. In 1935 the Philippines reached another milestone. It, at last, became a self–governing country. The Philippines remained a possession of the United States, but the Tydings–McDuffie Act of 1934 promised complete independence by 1946.

THE TYDINGS-MCDUFFIE ACT

The Tydings-McDuffie Act promised Filipino independence, but the real purpose of the law was to limit Filipino immigration into the United States. Previously, laws that excluded Asian immigration did not apply to Filipinos. As long as the Philippines was a colony of the United States, Filipinos could not be prevented from coming to the United States. Under the Tydings-McDuffie Act, however, Filipino immigration to the United States was limited to just fifty people per year. The Tydings-McDuffie Act brought a temporary stop to Filipino immigration. It was the result of a trend in the United States toward ethnic isolation and increasing discrimination against Filipino immigrants. Senator Millard Tydings defended the act by saying, "It is absolutely illogical to have an immigration policy to exclude Japanese and Chinese and permit Filipinos . . . to come into the country. . . . If they continue to settle in certain areas they will come in conflict with white labor . . . and increase the opportunity for more racial prejudice and bad feelings of all kinds."

In spite of the Philippines' newfound independence, hardships continued in the country. The government remained unstable, and many Filipinos dreamed of a better life. Furthermore, the U.S.-run schools were spreading propaganda. They taught Filipino students to accept the American way of life. The desire for greater opportunity, along with the teachings of American schools, caused many Filipinos to move to the United States.

Although the United States had passed a law in 1924 that stopped almost all Asian immigration, the law did not apply to Filipinos. Since the Philippines was a U.S. territory, Filipinos were allowed to travel back and forth.

While Filipinos were struggling with hardships in their homeland, many parts of the United States were facing a labor shortage. The 1924 law restricting immigration meant that farms, lumberyards, and canneries could no longer hire workers from overseas. The labor shortage led to the hiring of 4,000 to 5,000 Filipinos in cities such as Los Angeles, San Francisco, and Seattle. In addition to those hired to work in mainland fields, lumberyards, and canneries, about 120,000 Filipinos settled in Hawaii to work in the sugar and pineapple industries.

I did not know much about the United States, but I had heard...that there were many opportunities there. I had an American teacher who used to tell our class that in the United States, as long as you are willing to work and you are not weak, you can survive very well. So I was impressed with this. It was this kind of information that gave me all the courage.

—*Filipino immigrant A. B. Santos*

2

IN AMERICA

When Filipino immigrants arrived in the United States, they were eager to build a brighter future for themselves. But life in the new country was challenging. Filipinos did backbreaking work and faced many hardships. Still, the Filipinos were determined. They contributed a great deal to the United States and made the best of the opportunities they found.

SAKADAS

The first large Filipino immigration occurred in Hawaii. This group of immigrants had begun arriving in 1906, and their numbers steadily increased after the passage of the 1924 Immigration Act. They are sometimes called the first wave of Filipino immigrants (although small groups of Filipino students came before them).

Filipinos in Hawaii called themselves Sakadas, which means "contract workers" in their native language of Tagalog. Sakadas worked for five huge U.S.

companies that controlled Hawaii's sugar and pineapple industries. The companies hired their field-workers through the Hawaiian Sugar Planters' Association (HSPA), and the companies did not treat their employees very well.

Sakadas faced many challenges. They began working before sunup and put in eight- or nine-hour days. Their tasks included hoeing, weeding, cutting, loading, and hauling. The work was exhausting, and the pay was low. Sakadas did make more money than they could in their home country. However, life in Hawaii was more expensive than in the Philippines. The paychecks Sakadas worked so hard for quickly disappeared. Filipino immigrants had come to Hawaii with the promise of a better life.

CHECK OUT WWW.INAMERICABOOKS.COM FOR LINKS TO LEARN MORE ABOUT THE HISTORY OF FILIPINO IMMIGRATION INTO THE UNITED STATES.

PENSIONADOS

The first Filipinos officially admitted into the United States were pensionados—students who came to study with the help of pensions or small government scholarships. The U.S. government authorized the pensionado program on August 26, 1903, and began two months later when about 100 young Filipinos arrived in California. By 1905 *Filipino Students Magazine* was being published in Berkeley, California, and by 1912, 209 Filipino men and women had earned degrees or advanced their education at about fifty U.S. colleges and universities.

SAKADAS

In 1906 Albert F. Judd (a lawyer for the companies that controlled Hawaii's sugar and pineapple industries) spent six months in the Philippines trying to recruit Filipino workers. He could find only fifteen volunteers. On the afternoon of December 20, 1906, the ship *Doric* landed in Honolulu with the recruits, ranging in age from fourteen to fifty-six. They were all from the Ilocos region of northern Luzon. Although the Ilocano had a reputation for being willing travelers, only about one hundred more of them came to Hawaii in 1907. The main reason for the small number was that the HSPA would not pay for the return of the men after they had completed their three-year contract.

No recruiting was done in 1908, but in 1909 the HSPA tried new tactics. Filipinos were hired as recruiters. They were given ten to fifteen pesos (five to seven dollars) for each person they recruited. Starting in 1915, the HSPA paid the Sakadas' return fares and provided housing for them. The recruiters also went from town to town showing free, specially made movies that pictured the positive side to life in Hawaii. This recruiting campaign was highly successful.

But what they found was backbreaking labor, unexpected expenses, and inadequate pay.

CALIFORNIA DAYS

Life was no better for Filipinos in California and the Pacific Northwest than it was for those in Hawaii. California farmworkers did "stoop labor," which meant stooping down for ten hours each day to pick or cut fields full of lettuce, asparagus, cauliflower, peas, celery, beets, tomatoes, or

Filipino boys perform "stoop labor" on a lettuce farm in Imperial Valley, California.

spinach. In Oregon and Washington, workers harvested crops and worked in the lumber industry. Around Puget Sound in Washington, thousands of Filipinos worked in the salmon canneries.

No matter where they worked, Filipinos got low wages. Immigrants faced discrimination as well. While Filipinos in Hawaii found greater acceptance because of the large number of other Asians living on the islands, those in California and the Northwest often felt like outsiders. Many Americans treated Filipinos poorly. They did not let them rent rooms in good neighborhoods. Because they could not find good housing, Filipinos often lived in overcrowded conditions. In California's San Joaquin Valley, for example, sixty Filipinos lived together in a barn with twenty sleeping in the loft and forty on the barn floor.

In addition to these hardships, Filipinos faced unfair laws in their new country. In California and other western states, it was hard for professional Filipinos to get licenses as doctors, teachers, lawyers, engineers, and nurses. Another law prevented Filipinos from marrying whites. And in 1928, California congressional representative Richard J. Welch introduced a law to stop further Filipino immigration. Welch's law, however, did not pass. The tide of immigrants was difficult to stop because the California farmers and the Hawaiian sugar and pineapple growers needed workers.

Filipinos soon realized that laws could work for them as well as against them. They began to form agricultural unions, or groups that worked for the rights of farmworkers. The Filipino agricultural union movement started in 1930. Violence and strikes—protests in which laborers refuse to work—soon followed. There was a wave of race riots. Many Filipinos were beaten. Filipinos who stood up for themselves faced threats of violence and harassment.

> *My parents were sent to the Wailua Sugar and Pineapple Plantation. They lived in labor camps. . . . It was sad, because my father said that they were so mistreated by the different crew bosses. . . . They would leave for work before the break of dawn and return long after dusk. The women like my mother would do the cooking, and some of them would go to work in the fields along with the men.*
>
> —Filipino Connie Tirona, describing the hardships her parents experienced as laborers in Hawaii in the late 1920s

Immigrants did not have easy jobs on the farms. The work was physically demanding, and the immigrants were forced to work long hours with little pay.

Despite the dangers they faced, thousands of Filipinos united to form the Filipino Labor Union (FLU) in December 1933. The FLU worked toward several goals: a minimum wage of thirty-five cents an hour, an eight-hour workday, employment without regard to race, and acceptance of the union's power in hiring and in bargaining for workers' rights. But the Great Depression (1929–1942), a time of economic hardship, made achieving these goals difficult. Finally, about seven thousand Filipinos joined with white and Mexican workers to strike against the California lettuce industry in 1934. The lettuce farmers met some of the workers' demands, but conditions did not improve much until workers formed the Filipino Agricultural Laborers Association in 1938. By 1940 this multiracial organization had thirty thousand members in California alone.

ALASKEROS

Alaska was the third–largest Filipino population center in the United States after Hawaii and California. The number of Filipinos in Alaska at any given time varied, however, because of the seasonal nature of the work in the salmon canneries that employed them. Filipino workers stayed in Alaska from late spring to late summer, the seasons in which cannery work was available.

SAKADAS ON STRIKE

Field-workers in Hawaii participated in strikes much like the ones led by unions in California. But the Sakadas' lives did not improve for quite some time. It was only in the late 1930s that the unions finally gained pay raises and other improvements for field-workers. In 1950 the power of the five companies that controlled the sugar and pineapple industries was broken, along with the old plantation system that had exploited so many Filipinos and others. Also by the 1950s, many Filipinos had started their own businesses or entered the professions and had become respected middle-class citizens of Hawaii. In 1959 Filipinos in Hawaii became full-fledged citizens of the United States, when Hawaii became the fiftieth state in the union.

Filipino cannery workers pose outside their cannery in Alaska. In the late 1920s, thousands of Filipinos arrived each year to find work in the canneries.

Money was supposed to be easy to make in Alaska, but the pay was actually not much—forty-five dollars a month, or three hundred dollars for a six-month season. The cannery workers, who called themselves Alaskeros, worked from 6:00 A.M. to 6:00 P.M., hauling the salmon in from boats and onto trucks that took the fish to the canneries. Wearing rubber aprons and boots, the Alaskeros then hosed down the fish, sorted them out with hooks, cut off their heads and tails, cleaned them out, and cooked, canned, and sealed them. Other jobs included making wooden boxes and packing the cans for shipment south.

Because Alaska's population included native Alaskans (Eskimos) and other Asian workers, Filipinos faced less prejudice there than in California.

Nevertheless, injustices did occur in the big salmon canneries. Often Filipinos were not paid fairly for their work. By 1936 the Alaskeros had formed their first cannery workers' union.

Some of the Filipino cannery workers married Eskimos and made Alaska their permanent home. Soon they established communities that brought some stability to their lives. In 1935 the Filipinos formed a social club called the Filipino Community of Juneau. In 1930 there were 4,200 Alaskeros working in the canneries. By 1940 the number had grown to about 9,000. During that same year, the total Filipino

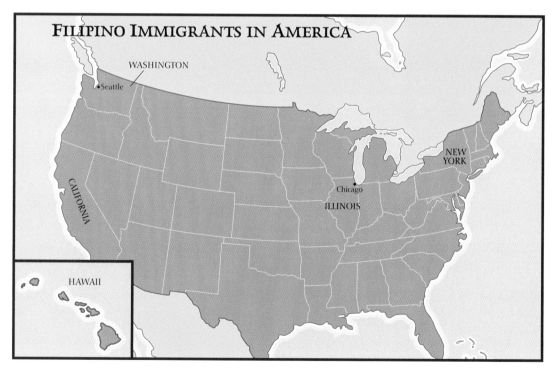

The largest number of Filipino immigrants in the United States have settled in California, but small Filipino communities can be found in many states. Visit www.inamericabooks.com to download this and other maps.

population of the United States was approximately 128,000, including 53,000 in the territory of Hawaii.

FILIPINO STUDENTS

Not all Filipinos came to the United States as laborers. Self-supporting students made up another group of Filipino immigrants. Self-supporting students did not come to the United States on scholarships. Instead, they found ways to pay for their education themselves. Most of the students were young, single males who first settled in college towns in the Midwest and the East. Chicago, Illinois, with its good schools, became the site of one of the earliest and largest concentrations of Filipinos. This was the start of the so-called Little Manilas in various cities.

PEDRO BLANCO

Pedro M. Blanco was a self-supporting student who landed in California in 1917. He had $3.50 in his pocket. Blanco got a job picking fruit and worked his way through both high school and his freshman year at the University of California. Later, he worked in the wheat fields of Kansas and earned enough money for a ticket to New York, where he entered Columbia University in 1922. During the summers, Blanco went from city to city selling Filipino hats and embroideries. He also made money for his education by giving lectures on the need for Philippine independence. Because he was such a good speaker, Blanco was invited to speak on the topic of Philippine independence in opposition to a former governor of Massachusetts. After several years of hard work, Blanco finally received a degree from the Columbia School of Business in 1924.

Eddie Maglaya (above), a self-supporting student, worked part-time as a butler while he attended Dunwoody Institute in Minnesota in the late 1920s.

The self-supporting students were flexible. They took whatever jobs they could to support themselves while going to school. Regardless of their abilities, it was hard for the students to find good jobs. Employers discriminated against them because of their race. Many students worked as hotel doorkeepers, bellhops, bus staff, kitchen helpers, domestic servants, waiters, cooks, and housepainters.

Filipino students set up social or educational clubs wherever they went. George Washington University in Washington, D.C., was home to a group called the Philippensians. Similar groups sprang up in Minnesota (Filipinosotans); Des Moines, Iowa; Kansas City, Kansas (Kansas City Filipinos); Moscow, Idaho (Filipino Idahoans); Ithaca, New York (Philippine Collegians);

Jonesboro, Arkansas; Angola, Indiana; Veronia, Oregon (Filipino Brotherhood); Lincoln, Nebraska; and Butte, Montana. Self-supporting students lived in Hawaii as well.

In order to help form an identity for themselves, Filipino students started their own newspapers and magazines. These periodicals often featured the successes of young Filipinos. An early Filipino American magazine called the *Republic*, for example, included stories of successful Filipino students on a special page titled "Making Good in the U.S." By the late 1930s, about fourteen

MANY PEOPLE ARE INTERESTED IN LEARNING ABOUT THEIR FAMILY'S HISTORY. THIS STUDY IS CALLED GENEALOGY. IF YOU'D LIKE TO LEARN ABOUT YOUR OWN GENEALOGY AND HOW YOUR ANCESTORS CAME TO AMERICA, VISIT WWW.INAMERICABOOKS.COM FOR TIPS AND LINKS TO HELP GET YOU STARTED. THERE YOU'LL ALSO FIND TIPS ON RESEARCHING NAMES IN YOUR FAMILY HISTORY.

thousand self-supporting students had come to the United States. The students contributed a great deal to their communities while furthering their education.

3

WORLD WAR II
TO THE
THIRD WAVE

Many young Filipinos found that the easiest way to see the world—and especially the United States—was to sign up with the armed services. With the start of World War II (1939–1945), large numbers of Filipinos joined the military. Filipinos who joined the military got the support of many Americans. When Filipinos showed that they were willing to fight alongside U.S. soldiers, the United States at last began to give Filipinos the respect they deserved.

FILIPINO SOLDIERS

World War II—a conflict in which the United States and other countries fought against Japan, Italy, and Germany—came to the Philippines just hours after it came to the United States. Shortly after bombing Pearl Harbor in Hawaii on December 7, 1941, Japan attacked Manila. Two weeks later, Japan invaded the Philippines at Lingayen on Luzon. Thousands of Filipino Americans wanted to fight against the Japanese in order to help both the United States and the country of their ancestors. In California alone, about sixteen thousand Filipinos signed up for the first draft. The problem was that under a 1940 law called the Selective Service Act, only U.S. citizens were allowed to serve in the armed forces. Most Filipinos living in the United States were nationals—neither citizens nor aliens (people who belong to another country or government). Because of their status, they were also not allowed to work in defense factories.

Many Filipino Americans believed they should have the right to defend their country. They wrote letters of protest to the secretary of war and to President Franklin D. Roosevelt. The letters worked. On December 20, 1941, President Roosevelt gave Filipinos the right both to serve in the armed forces and to work in defense factories.

In April 1942, Filipinos formed the First Filipino Infantry Battalion. Lieutenant Colonel Robert H. Offley was in charge of the battalion. Offley spoke fluent Tagalog because he had spent his youth on Mindoro, where his father was governor. Many Filipino officers and men were under Offley's command. The battalion was so large that it was reorganized into the First Filipino Regiment and Band. This larger group had 143 officers, 6 warrant officers, and 3,019 men, all Filipinos. On November 21, 1942, Filipinos formed a second group called the Second Filipino Infantry Regiment.

The men of the two Filipino regiments were trained for jungle warfare so they could lead the way in recapturing the Philippines from the Japanese. Many were already familiar with the land but were given special instruction in intelligence (gathering military information), the Japanese language, radio communications, judo (a style of fighting), mapmaking, demolition, booby traps, and survival.

A HISTORY OF SERVICE

Even before World War II, Filipinos were serving in the U.S. Navy. Many young men joined the military before the United States passed the Selective Service Act. Filipino recruits signed up at the U.S. naval base at Cavite, across the bay from Manila.

Two Filipino sailors pose aboard their ship in 1940.

They typically served as cooks, waiters, dishwashers, and custodians. The work was hard, but the pay was good. The best thing about joining the service was that after three years in the navy or marines, the men could become U.S. citizens. Many went beyond this limit and made twenty-year careers out of the navy, retiring with benefits.

Not all Filipinos in the navy remained in service jobs. Some advanced because of their own special abilities. Filipino sailor Leon Morales, for example, was in charge of the financial records and daily funds for his ship. Morales's superior officer praised him as "exceptionally capable, accurate and honest."

Filipino American soldiers stand at attention under the U.S. flag in Manila, the Philippines.

At different times during the war, the regiments were sent to Australia, the Philippines, and New Guinea. Before going overseas on February 20, 1943, 1,200 of the men stood proudly in a V formation on the Camp Beale parade grounds. In a radio–broadcasted ceremony, the men became U.S. citizens. Similar ceremonies took place wherever Filipinos served.

A select group of men from the regiments formed the First Reconnaissance Battalion (Special). This was a commando unit, or a group specially trained to raid enemy territory. During the campaign to retake the Philippines, the commandos parachuted or went by submarine into key areas. They disguised themselves as village traders or other local people but secretly gathered information about the Japanese. They radioed this information back to other U.S. troops near the area or to Australia at a rate of nearly four thousand messages a month. The commandos also destroyed Japanese communications lines.

Other Filipino American soldiers were called coast watchers. They radioed important information on enemy ship movements and weather conditions that affected military operations. This work was dangerous, since the watchers were sometimes under enemy fire. Members of the first and second regiments also served in the parachute–naval assault to recapture the island of Corregidor in 1944.

The Filipino American volunteers succeeded in liberating the Philippines from Japan. Many of these brave men earned the Bronze Star and other medals. Among them were several from California, Staff Sergeant Paulino A. Rosales, Stockton; Corporal Ralph M. Balunes, Los Angeles; and Technician Teodore M. Taluban, Salinas.

In addition to the Filipino troops on land, about fifteen thousand Filipinos served above and beneath the sea, in ships and on submarines. They also volunteered for the marines and the coast guard. An uncounted number of Filipinos served in the Army Air Corps as everything from clerks to airplane mechanics.

At home in the United States, Filipinos served as members of Filipino units in the California State Militia. Others worked in California and Washington aircraft factories or raised money for the war effort.

Filipino Americans who fought in World War II join friends to celebrate the end of the war.

JEEPNEYS

Back in the Philippines, one outgrowth of World War II was that thousands of U.S. army jeeps were repainted and turned into taxi cabs.

Filipinos made the jeeps longer and decorated them with silver foil, miniature animals, tassels, and folk and religious art. Filipinos call these special cabs jeepneys *(right)*. Jeepneys can be seen all over the streets in the Philippines. They share the crowded cities with cars, buses, trucks, and bicycles. The colorful and reliable jeepneys are a symbol of the Philippines. They are also a symbol of the versatility and energy of the Filipino people, both in the Philippines and the United States.

After the War

By the end of World War II, the United States was slowly gaining more respect for Filipino Americans. Filipinos had fought for democracy in the war, and Americans finally began to recognize their contributions. In 1941 Washington State gave Filipino nationals the right to own property. California did the same in 1943. And on July 2, 1946, two days before the Philippines achieved full independence, President Harry S. Truman signed the Filipino Naturalization Act.

This act gave all Filipinos who lived in the United States the right to become U.S. citizens. The law opened up new possibilities for Filipinos to seek equality.

In 1946 the United States passed the War Brides Act. This act allowed Filipinos who served in the U.S. armed forces in the Philippines and who had married there to bring their wives and children to the United States. The same law allowed the immigration of former Philippine Scouts (soldiers who served under U.S. officers in the Philippines during the territorial period), along with their wives and children. Because of this law, California's Filipino population more than doubled between 1940

THE RESCISSION ACT

While the 1940s brought some improvements to the lives of Filipino immigrants—particularly those who served in World War II—Filipino Americans still faced a great deal of discrimination. As American nationals, Filipino soldiers had been promised the same health and pension benefits as any other soldier who fought for the United States. In 1946, however, Congress passed the Rescission Act. This act made it legal to deprive Filipino soldiers of benefits. After the passage of the Rescission Act, Filipino veterans came to the United States in order to fight for their benefits. But Congress did not respond.

The struggle continues in modern times. Filipino veterans still aren't afforded the same rights as others who served in World War II. Because of their situation, Filipinos who fought in the war are sometimes known as "second-class veterans."

and 1960. It went from about thirty-one thousand to about sixty-five thousand. In 1948 Filipino Americans in California gained another legal right—they were no longer prevented from marrying whites.

Filipinos who arrived in the United States between 1950 and 1960 are considered the second wave of immigrants. As the Filipino population in the United States increased, new employment opportunities opened up. In contrast to the first wave of Filipinos, who were largely agricultural laborers, the newer immigrants were able to find jobs in the aircraft, electronics, and chemical industries. New laws helped

Interracial marriages became more common among Filipino immigrants after 1948. This couple was photographed in 1954.

lift racial barriers in government jobs, attracting Filipinos and also encouraging private businesses to hire them.

Another major turning point for Filipinos and other minorities occurred in 1948. That year President Truman ordered an end to discrimination in the U.S. armed forces. Because of this measure, Filipinos in the navy were no longer restricted to low-level positions. By the mid-1980s, there were about four hundred Filipino officers in the U.S. Navy.

FIND LINKS TO LEARN MORE ABOUT VARIOUS IMMIGRATION LAWS AND HOW THEY HAVE AFFECTED THE FILIPINO AMERICAN COMMUNITY AT WWW.INAMERICABOOKS.COM.

THE THIRD WAVE

After World War II, large numbers of Filipinos came to California under the War Brides Act and other special laws. A new immigration law, however, signed on July 4, 1946 (the date of Philippine independence), limited the number of additional Filipinos who could come to the United States to one hundred per year. The quota was a hardship for Filipinos who wanted to immigrate but who were not covered by the War Brides Act.

In 1965, at the foot of the Statue of Liberty, President Lyndon B. Johnson signed a new immigration law that put an

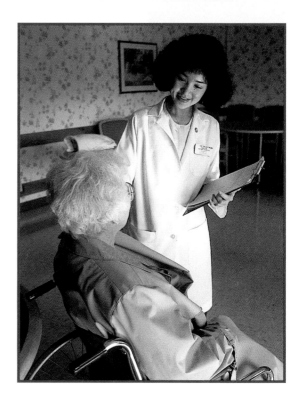

After President Lyndon B. Johnson signed a new immigration act into law in 1965, many Filipinos in skilled professions, such as nursing, entered the United States.

end to the old system, which was based on varying quotas for individual countries. Instead, a yearly world quota of immigrants was set at 290,000, with no individual country allowed to send more than 20,000 immigrants in one year. The increase in Filipino immigrants was immediate. Between 1961 and 1985, nearly 683,000 Filipinos came to make new homes in the United States. These newcomers made up the third wave of Filipino immigration.

Ferdinand E. Marcos

The new law favored the entry of relatives of people already in the United States and of professionals such as doctors, lawyers, engineers, nurses, pharmacists, scientists, and people in technical fields. Filipinos in these professions, both men and women, came to the United States. They came for many reasons—to improve their technical skills, to study on scholarships, to join their families, to get married, and for financial reasons.

Politics also contributed to the third wave of immigration. In 1965

Ferdinand E. Marcos became president of the Philippines. Marcos's first term as president was successful. He improved the country's economy and encouraged the use of a crop known as miracle rice. Miracle rice was disease-resistant. Marcos promised that it would increase the Philippines' rice crop. In the 1969 election, Marcos received a large vote. He became the first Philippine president to win a second term. But this term did not go smoothly. The country suffered more economic problems. The miracle rice did not produce extra crops as Marcos had said it would. And adding to the unrest was the rise of a group called the New People's Army, a group that believed in the political philosophy of Communism. Marcos blamed the unrest on the Communists. He declared martial law and began censoring the press, radio, and television. In January 1973, the Philippines got a new constitution. The constitution gave Marcos absolute power.

FIND LINKS TO READ THE LATEST FILIPINO NEWS AT WWW.INAMERICABOOKS.COM.

Political unrest continued through the 1980s to the early 2000s. Poverty, explosive population growth, and unequal distribution of wealth caused many Filipinos to seek new lives in the United States. Filipinos have become the largest Asian

VOTING AND CITIZENSHIP

The Citizenship Retention and Re-acquisition Act of 2003 (also known as the Philippines Republic Act No. 9225) gave Filipino Americans the right to claim citizenship in both the United States and the Philippines. It also gave them the right to vote in all national elections held in the Philippines. Filipino Americans first took advantage of their right to vote in Filipino national elections in the year 2004. They cast their ballots from their homes in the United States, and Gloria Macapagal-Arroyo was voted into a second term as the president of the Republic of the Philippines.

immigrant group in the United States. They work in many different professions, and they contribute a great deal to the communities in which they live.

CUSTOMS AND TRADITIONS

Filipino Americans bring many customs and traditions to the United States. As a group, however, Filipinos have had some difficulty preserving their ethnic identity. The Philippines is steeped in the traditions of its Spanish and American occupiers. As a result, the country has lost some of its native heritage. Filipino immigrants do not share a single culture or language. They tend not to establish the close-knit communities that bind other immigrant groups. While the absence of a strong group identity makes it difficult for Filipino immigrants to stay in touch with their native culture, it can also make it easier for them to integrate into U.S. society.

Because the United States occupied the Philippine Islands,

When I was younger, I used to question my identity. I remember asking mom or dad, "Am I Filipino? Am I American?" ... "American Filipino" is what I would say now. American because I was born here, and Filipino because I am of Filipino descent. That's my interpretation.

—Anamaria Labao Cabato, on her cultural identity

Filipino immigrants are well acquainted with U.S. culture. American music, movies, and brand names are everywhere in the Philippines. Furthermore, Filipinos speak English fluently. The Philippines is the third-largest English-speaking country in the world (after the United States and the United Kingdom). As a result, Filipino immigrants arrive to their new home without having to overcome a language barrier. Filipinos also tend to be very educated. Education is important in the Filipino culture. About 40 percent of Filipino Americans are college graduates. Because Filipino immigrants are often well educated, they find it easier than many other Asian immigrants to find jobs in technical fields, such as health care. Unlike many other Asian immigrant groups, Filipino immigrants share the religious beliefs and values of the majority of native-born Americans. Most Filipinos are Roman Catholic, so they tend to blend in easily with The United States' primarily Judeo–Christian society.

DISCRIMINATION IN THE WORKPLACE

Filipino immigrants tend to be highly qualified and educated workers, but they still face racial discrimination in the workplace. While Filipino American health care workers tend to be well paid, those in other industries do not get the same salaries and benefits as white workers. Filipino American engineers and architects are paid less than white workers with the same skills and abilities. Those in the corporate and hospitality industries face economic inequalities as well. Many Filipino Americans are fighting to get the same pay and benefits as their white counterparts. They are striving for fair and equal treatment in all industries.

Education is an important part of Filipino culture, and Filipinos boast a higher percentage of college graduates than many other immigrant groups.

Since Filipinos tend not to stand out in the United States, Filipino Americans are sometimes known as the "invisible minority." Most Americans are familiar with Chinese and Vietnamese immigrants, but they often don't know as much about Filipinos. Many Filipino immigrants are working to increase awareness about the Philippines and its people. They encourage Filipino Americans to celebrate their group's contributions to the United States. In 2002 Filipino Americans made a remarkable stride in their campaign to educate others about their culture. That year marked the opening of the Filipino Community Center in Waipahu, Hawaii. The Filipino Community Center is the largest Filipino American institution in the United States. Its goals are to teach people about Filipino American culture and history, and to provide cultural, social, and economic services to the Filipino American community.

In spite of the difficulties Filipino Americans face when it comes to promoting awareness about their culture, Filipino immigrants bring many rich traditions to the communities in which they live. As in almost every culture, food is important to Filipinos' ethnic identity. Filipino cuisine has both Spanish and Asian influences. Foods such as steamed rice, *misua* (thin noodles), and *lumpia* (light, crispy egg rolls) are popular, as are Spanish cooking methods such as *adobado* (marinading) and *guisado* (sautéing). A traditional Filipino drink is *salabat*. Salabat is a hot tea made with gingerroot and sugar. Many Filipinos also enjoy *halo-halo*. Halo–halo is a milk shake usually made from ten different ingredients, including coconut, sweet red beans, egg custard, and milk.

Halo-halo is a common Filipino treat.

CHICKEN ADOBO

This recipe is a favorite throughout the Philippines and is still prepared by many Filipino Americans. To learn how to prepare other Filipino dishes, visit www.inamericabooks.com for links.

8 WHOLE CHICKEN LEGS, CUT INTO DRUMSTICK AND THIGH SECTIONS

1 1/2 CUP DISTILLED WHITE VINEGAR

3 GARLIC CLOVES, CRUSHED

2 BAY LEAVES

1/2 TABLESPOON WHOLE BLACK PEPPERCORNS, LIGHTLY CRUSHED

1 CUP WATER

3/4 CUP SOY SAUCE

3 TABLESPOONS VEGETABLE OIL

COOKED WHITE RICE AS AN ACCOMPANIMENT

1. In a large kettle, combine chicken, vinegar, garlic, bay leaves, peppercorns, and water.
2. Bring the mixture to a boil and simmer it, covered, for 20 minutes.
3. Add soy sauce and simmer the mixture, covered, for 20 minutes.
4. Use tongs to transfer the chicken to a plate and boil the liquid for 10 minutes.
5. Let the sauce cool, removing the bay leaves and using a spoon to skim the fat from the surface of the sauce.
6. In a large skillet, heat oil over high heat until it is hot but not smoking. Sauté the chicken in the oil, turning it for five minutes, or until it is browned.
7. Transfer the chicken to a platter that is high enough to keep the sauce from running over the top, pour the sauce over it, and serve chicken with rice.

Serves 4 to 8

Religious celebrations are important to many Filipino Americans. Their Roman Catholic faith often plays a prominent role in their lives. In the Philippines, people throw big parties on occasions such as baptisms, weddings, and confirmations. Many Filipino immigrants carry this tradition over to the United States. The most important days for Filipinos include Easter, Holy Week (the week before Easter), and Christmas. At Christmastime, it is customary to attend church on each day throughout the week leading up to Christmas. The most important event of the week is the Misa de Gallo, or the midnight Christmas Eve church service. At this service, Filipinos celebrate the birth of Jesus Christ. In the days before

Filipino men and women join in song at a Filipino Christmas celebration in Honolulu, Hawaii.

the Misa de Gallo, Filipinos traditionally create lanterns out of colored crepe paper. The lanterns are called *parols*. Filipinos hold competitions to see who can build the best parol. Christmas festivities also include a *panunuluyan*, or a walk through the streets in which a woman dressed as Mary and a man dressed as Joseph act out the story of Jesus' birth. The Filipino Christmas celebration goes on into January. At this time, church services remind Filipinos of the importance of charity and understanding. The Feast of El Niño is the culmination of the holiday. The Feast of El Niño ends with a procession in which the baby Jesus is brought to the church.

In addition to religious celebrations, many Filipino Americans participate in community festivals that celebrate the Filipino culture. Most of these festivals take place in May, which is Asian Pacific American Heritage Month. One such celebration is the Festival of Philippine Arts & Culture. This annual event, held

in San Pedro, California, showcases the work of Filipino artists from around the country. Other cultural celebrations include the Filipino Fiesta and Parade, held in Honolulu, Hawaii, and the Filipino Festival, which takes place in New Orleans,

Filipino children participate in the Philippine Independence Day Celebration in New York City. Filipino Americans gather at the festival each year to celebrate the Philippines' independence from Spain. Check out www.inamericabooks.com for links to locate Filipino events and activities in your area.

Louisiana. At these festivals, Filipino Americans enjoy celebrating and learning more about their Filipino heritage.

Music and dance are some other important aspects of Filipino culture. A traditional folk dance called the *fandango saw ila* reminds Filipino Americans of their heritage, as does the *tinikling*, a difficult dance in which two people hold the ends of two bamboo poles and clink the poles together in time to the music while a dancer hops between the moving poles. Another popular Filipino dance is called *binasuan*, which means "with use of a drinking glass." In this dance, dancers show off their balancing skills by moving to the music as

Girls from a traditional Filipino dance group practice the binasuan dance before performing in a parade in New York City.

glasses filled with rice wine rest on their heads and in the palms of their hands. The dancers perform fast turns, sit down, and even roll on the floor—all without spilling a drop of wine! Sometimes, Filipino American celebrations also include a *rondalla*, or a traditional Filipino string band.

Filipino Americans bring a variety of traditions to the United States. By connecting with their cultural heritage and embracing their identity as Americans, they build bridges between their history and their future.

FIND LINKS TO DISCOVER MORE ABOUT THE MANY WAYS THAT PEOPLE OF FILIPINO HERITAGE CONTRIBUTE TO LIFE IN AMERICA AT WWW.INAMERICABOOKS.COM.

FAMOUS FILIPINO AMERICANS

JOSÉ ARUEGO (b. 1932) Born in Manila, the Philippines, Aruego is known as one of the best American graphic artists and illustrators of children's books. Aruego started out as a lawyer in the Philippines but came to New York City to study graphic arts and advertising at Parsons School of Design. After graduation, Aruego drew cartoons for the *Saturday Evening Post, Look*, and other magazines. In 1969 Aruego published his first children's book, *The King and His Friends*. Since then he has illustrated many popular books for young people, including *Leo the Late Bloomer, Juan and the Asuangs*, and *Where Are You Going, Little Mouse?*

TAI BABILONIA (b. 1959) Babilonia was born in Hollywood,

 California, to an American mother and a Filipino father. She is an outstanding figure skater who competed in the Olympic Games.

Babilonia started skating at the age of six. At the age of eight, she was teamed with ten–year–old Randy Gardner. The pair soon started training with a professional coach. In 1976 Babilonia and Gardner placed fifth in the Olympics. In 1979 they became the first Americans in twenty–nine years to win the World Skating Pairs Championship. They looked like sure winners for the gold medal in the 1980 Olympics, but Gardner pulled a muscle during training, shattering their hopes for top honors. Babilonia went on to become a star with the Ice Capades. She and Gardner served as official hosts for *Sports Illustrated* in the 2002 Winter Olympics in Salt Lake City, Utah.

DIOSDADO BANATAO (b. 1946) Banatao (often known by his nickname, Dado) is a highly accomplished businessperson and engineer. Born in Cagayan Province, the Philippines, Banatao immigrated to the United States in 1968. Banatao is the managing partner of the company Tallwood Venture Capital. As an engineer, he has developed many new technologies. Banatao earned degrees in electrical engineering and computer science from Stanford University in California and the Mapúa Institute of Technology in the Philippines. He lives in Silicon Valley, California, and is married with three children.

ANGELA PEREZ BARAQUIO

(b. 1976) Baraquio (now Angela Perez Baraquio Grey) was born in Hawaii. On October 14, 2000, she became the first Filipino American to be

crowned Miss America. Baraquio graduated from Moanalua High School with high academic honors. She then earned a degree in

elementary education from the University of Hawaii at Manoa. Baraquio went on to become a teacher at Holy Family Catholic Academy in Honolulu. She also coached track, volleyball, and basketball. Baraquio returned to the University of Hawaii at Manoa for a master's degree in education administration. She plans to work as a school administrator in Hawaii.

CARLOS BULOSAN (1913–1956)

Bulosan was born in a farming village near the town of Binalonan and spent his first seventeen years in the Philippines. In 1930 he traveled to the United States in search of a better life. Bulosan worked in an Alaskan salmon cannery and as a migrant farmer, moving from place to place to find work. Frustrated by the backbreaking labor and discrimination he faced, Bulosan began to write about his experiences. Bulosan's book *America Is in the Heart* expressed the disappointment and heartbreak felt by many Filipino immigrants. His work is an accurate and moving description of the early Filipino American experience.

TIA CARRERE (b. 1967) Carrere is

an actress, singer, and model. Born in Honolulu, Hawaii, Carrere is of Filipino, Chinese, and Spanish descent. Carrere made her acting debut in the movie *Aloha Summer*. She then moved to Los Angeles, where she landed a role in the popular soap opera *General Hospital*. In 1992

Carrere took on the role of rock singer Cassandra in *Wayne's World*. As

Cassandra, Carrere performed all her own songs. From 1999 to 2002, Carrere played Professor Sydney Fox in the television series *Relic Hunter*. She was also the voice of the character Nani in the 2002 film *Lilo & Stitch*.

BENJAMIN J. CAYETANO (b. 1939) Born in Hawaii, Cayetano grew up in a Filipino neighborhood west of downtown Honolulu. Cayetano attended Loyola Law School in Los Angeles, California, and earned his degree in 1971. After graduation, Cayetano returned to Hawaii and ran for the Hawaii State House of Representatives. In 1978 he was elected to the Hawaii State Senate. In 1994 Cayetano was nominated to run for governor of Hawaii. He won the seat, becoming the first Filipino American to be elected as a governor.

NATALIE COUGHLIN (b. 1982) Coughlin is a native of Concord,

California. She is partly of Filipino ancestry. Her grandmother is from Meycauayan, Bulacan. Coughlin is a swimmer who was part of the 2004 Olympic swimming team for the United States. She won a gold medal at the 2004 Summer Olympics in the women's 100-meter backstroke. Coughlin also helped her team win a silver medal in the women's 4-x-100-meter freestyle relay. Before traveling to Athens, Greece, for the Olympic Games, Coughlin was a student and athlete at the University of California, Berkeley.

JOCELYN ENRIQUEZ (b. 1974) Enriquez was born and raised in San Francisco, California. A talented singer and performer, she became the first Filipino American to make it in the mainstream music industry. Enriquez started singing as a young girl. She performed in the San Francisco Girls Chorus and in a band managed by her parents. In 1994 Enriquez released the album *Lovely*, featuring the dance hits "I've Been Thinking about You" and "Make This Last Forever." In 1997 she released the self-titled *Jocelyn*, on which she recorded a song in the language of Tagalog.

ROMAN GABRIEL (b. 1940) Born in Wilmington, North Carolina, Gabriel is a well-known

Filipino American athlete. In high school, Gabriel was a triple-letter winner in sports and an excellent student. He received about fifty scholarship offers and chose to attend college at North Carolina State. The six-foot four-inch, 220-pound Gabriel was drafted by the Los Angeles Rams football team in 1962. He was All-Pro for eleven years. In 1969 Gabriel was named the NFL's Most Valuable Player and Player of the Year. In 1973 he joined the Philadelphia Eagles and finished his career with them in 1977.

JESSICA HAGEDORN (b. 1949)

Hagedorn was born in Manila, the Philippines, and came to the United States in 1960. A talented writer, performance artist, and musician, Hagedorn published her first book of

poems in 1972, when she was only twenty years old. Hagedorn has written many works, including *Danger and Beauty*, a much-talked-about collection of stories and poems. In 1993 Hagedorn edited a book entitled *Charlie Chan Is Dead: An Anthology of Contemporary Asian American Fiction*.

Hagedorn lives in New York and is married with two daughters.

LARRY DULAY ITLIONG

(1914–1977) Born in the Philippines, Itliong immigrated to the United States in 1929. Although he never finished elementary school, Itliong educated himself through hard work and determination. Itliong quickly became involved in workers' rights struggles in California and Alaska. In 1956 he founded the Filipino Farm Labor Union in California. Itliong led a strike of Filipino American farm workers in the grape vineyards in 1965. He was the area director of the Agricultural Workers Organizing Committee, or AWOC. Itliong's struggle for workers' rights inspired laborers everywhere to fight for better working conditions.

PABLO MANLAPIT (1891–1969)

A native of Lipa, Batangas, the Philippines, Manlapit came to Hawaii in 1910 as a laborer. Like other Sakadas, Manlapit worked as a field hand, but he was promoted to foreman and then to timekeeper. Manlapit was disturbed by the working conditions he saw in the fields. He led labor strikes and was fired from the plantation. In 1913–1914, Manlapit organized the Filipino Unemployment Association. In 1920 he helped launch a Hawaii-wide strike for better wages and working conditions. Manlapit also studied law. He was the first Filipino in Hawaii to pass the law examinations.

IRENE NATIVIDAD (b. 1948)

Natividad was born in Manila, the Philippines. She is an educator and an activist who works for the rights of women and Asian Americans. Natividad speaks many languages, including French, Italian, Tagalog, and Greek. She graduated first in her class from Long Island University in New York and went on to earn two master's degrees. Natividad began working as an English instructor in 1974. In 1984 she worked as the Asian American representative for the vice-presidential campaign of Geraldine Ferraro. Ferraro was the first woman to run for vice president of the United States. In 1985 Natividad was elected chair of the National Women's Political Caucus. She was the first Asian American to head a national women's organization.

LOU DIAMOND PHILLIPS

(b. 1962) Lou Diamond Phillips is an actor who was born at Subic Bay Naval Station in the Philippines. He studied drama and film technique at the University of Texas. Phillips is best known for his role as singer Ritchie Valens in the 1987 film *La Bamba*. He also played high school

student Angel Guzman in the film *Stand and Deliver* and Sergeant Monfriez in the military drama *Courage under Fire*. In addition to his roles on the big screen, Phillips had a part in the television series *Wolf Lake* and made a cameo appearance in the popular show *24*.

MANUEL QUEZON (1878–1944)

Born on Luzon, Quezon was a Filipino patriot who paved the way for his country's independence. Quezon fought in the revolt against the United States, and in 1907 he became the majority leader of the first Philippine Assembly under

U.S. rule. From 1909 to 1916, Quezon served as the Filipino resident commissioner in Washington, D.C. Quezon was instrumental in the passage of the Jones Act. This act, which passed in 1916, granted independence to the Filipinos. After the passage of the Jones Act, Quezon returned to the Philippines where he was elected president of the Philippine senate. As president of the senate, Quezon negotiated the Tydings–McDuffie Act with U.S. Senator Millard Tydings. In 1935 Quezon was elected president of the Commonwealth of the Philippines .

LEA SALONGA (b. 1971) Salonga was born in Manila, the Philippines, and began her acting career at the age of seven when she starred in the play *The King and I*. She began her music career at the age of ten

when she recorded the album *Small Voice*. In 1989 Salonga was selected to play the role of Kim in the musical *Miss Saigon*. She won several

awards for this performance. Salonga was the singing voice of Jasmine in the movie *Aladdin* and of

Fa Mulan in the film *Mulan*. In 2001 Salonga took on the role of Lien Hughes on the soap opera *As the World Turns*.

LALAINE VERGARA-PARAS

(b. 1987) Vergara–Paras (who is often known only as Lalaine) is a young actress whose parents were born in the Philippines. She grew up in California and made her acting debut playing Cosette in a Broadway production of *Les Miserables*. In addition to many other roles, Vergara–Paras

portrayed Miranda Sanchez on the television show *Lizzie McGuire* and the orphan Kate in the Disney Channel's version of *Annie*. Vergara–Paras is also a singer. She recorded an album entitled *Inside Story*, and she wrote several of the songs on the album herself.

TIMELINE

1500 B.C.	The first wave of Malays arrives in the region that would later become the Philippines.
300–200 B.C.	The Iron Age Malays arrive in the region that would later become the Philippines.
A.D. 1293	The Majapahit Empire arises in the Philippines region.
1565	The Spanish set up a permanent settlement in the Philippines region.
1896	The Filipinos revolt against the Spanish.
1898	Spain and the United States sign the Treaty of Paris, which gives the United States control over the Philippines.
1906–1934	The first major wave of Filipino immigrants arrives in Hawaii. Immigration increases and spreads to places such as California, Alaska, and the Pacific Northwest.
1934	Filipinos join Mexican and white workers in the California lettuce industry strike.
1935	The Philippines becomes a self-governing country.
1938	Filipino American laborers form the Filipino Agricultural Laborers Association.
1941	Japan attacks the Philippine capital of Manila. Thousands of Filipino Americans register for the draft.
1946	President Harry S. Truman signs the Filipino Naturalization Act, which gives Filipinos who live in the United States the right to become U.S. citizens. Carlos Bulosan's book *America Is in the Heart* is published. The Philippines gains full independence.

1950–1960	The second wave of Filipino immigrants move to the United States.
1956	Larry Dulay Itliong founds the Filipino Farm Labor Union in California.
1961–1985	Nearly 683,000 Filipino immigrants move to the United States, making up the third major wave of Filipino immigrants.
1965	Ferdinand E. Marcos becomes president of the Philippines.
1994	Benjamin J. Cayetano becomes governor of Hawaii.
2000	About 2.4 million people with Filipino ancestry are living in the United States.
2003	The Citizenship Retention and Re-acquisition Act gives Filipino Americans the right to dual citizenship and to vote in the Philippines' national elections.
2004	Typhoons hit the Philippines. Filipino Americans listen to news reports about the storms. Floods and landslides caused by the storms leave tens of thousands without homes. President Gloria Macapagal-Arroyo wins a second term as president of the Republic of the Philippines.

GLOSSARY

ANCESTOR: a family member from whom a person is descended

BUDDHIST: a person who follows the teachings of Gautama Buddha. Buddhism is a religion of eastern and central Asia.

COLONY: a country that is tied to or controlled by another country

CONVERT: to bring someone over from one viewpoint or belief to another

DIALECT: a regional variety of a language

EXPEDITION: a journey taken for a specific purpose

IMMIGRATE: to move to live in a country other than one's homeland. A person who immigrates is called an immigrant.

MIGRANT: a person who moves regularly from one region to another

MISSIONARY: a person on a religious mission, generally to promote a particular type of religion

PENSION: a sum of money that is paid regularly to a person

PLANTATION: a large estate on which crops are grown, usually with the help of peasant farmers or slave labor

QUOTA: a limit. Quotas on immigration to the United States set limits on the number of immigrants allowed to enter the United States.

SCHOLARSHIP: money given to students to help them pay for school

STRIKE: refusing to work until an employer agrees to meet certain conditions

THINGS TO SEE AND DO

FESTIVAL OF PHILIPPINE ARTS &
CULTURE, SAN PEDRO, CALIFORNIA
http://www.filamarts.org
This annual festival showcases the
work of Filipino artists and
celebrates the heritage of Filipino
Americans.

FILIPINO AMERICAN HISTORICAL
SOCIETY OF CHICAGO, CHICAGO,
ILLINOIS
http://www.fahsc.org
Founded in 1986, this center is
dedicated to preserving the history
of Chicago's Filipino American
community. The center provides
exhibits that tell the story of Filipino
Americans and offers education to
promote interest in Filipino heritage.

THE FILIPINO AMERICAN LIBRARY,
LOS ANGELES, CALIFORNIA
http://www.filipinoamericanlibrary.org
The Filipino American Library
promotes the culture, history, and
achievements of Filipino Americans.
It hosts art exhibits, film screenings,
and other events.

THE FILIPINO HERITAGE MUSEUM,
JERSEY CITY, NEW JERSEY
http://www.koleksyon.com/
filipinoheritagemuseum.asp
This museum celebrates the people
and culture of the Philippines.

THE NEWBERRY LIBRARY, CHICAGO,
ILLINOIS
http://www.newberry.org/nl/
newberryhome.html
The Newberry Library houses a
large collection of materials on both
the Philippines and Filipino
Americans. Information on
researching Filipino heritage can be
found at the library.

SOURCE NOTES

19   Bernard Reines, *A People's Hero: Rizal of the Philippines* (New York: Praeger Publishers, 1971), 95.

21   Yen Le Espiritu, *Filipino American Lives* (Philadelphia: Temple University Press, 1995), 3.

22   Lan Cao and Himilce Novas, *Everything You Need to Know about Asian-American History* (New York: Plume, 1996), 172.

23   Espiritu, 38.

28   Ibid., 66.

29   Frank H. Winter, *The Filipinos in America* (Minneapolis: Lerner Publications Company, 1988), 38.

38   Ibid., 42.

43   Alexandra Bandon, *Filipino Americans* (New York: New Discovery Books, 1993), 36–37.

47   Espiritu, 153.

SELECTED BIBLIOGRAPHY

Cao, Lan, and Himilce Novas. *Everything You Need to Know about Asian-American History.* New York: Plume, 1996. **This book provides an overview of important people, places, and dates in Asian American history.**

Central Intelligence Agency. "Philippines." *The World Factbook 2004.* http://www.cia.gov/cia/publications/factbook (November 10, 2004). **This document includes information on the Philippines' geography, people, government, economy, and history.**

Espiritu, Yen Le. *Filipino American Lives.* Philadelphia: Temple University Press, 1995. **This book explores Filipino American history and culture through the first-person narratives of several Filipino Americans.**

Kim, Hyung–Chan, ed. *Dictionary of Asian American History.* Westport, CT: Greenwood Press, 1986. **This book gives an overview of important people and events in the history of Asian Americans.**

Lai, Eric, and Dennis Arguelles, eds. *The New Face of Asian Pacific America: Numbers, Diversity, & Change in the 21st Century.* San Francisco: AsianWeek, 2003. **This book discusses the social conditions, ethnic identity, population, and statistics of several Asian Pacific immigrant groups.**

Library of Congress. "A Country Study: Philippines." *Country Studies.* October 2004. http://lcweb2.loc.gov/frd/cs/phtoc.html (November 10, 2004). **The Library of Congress describes and analyzes the politics, economy, and culture of the Philippines.**

Peplow, Evelyn. *The Philippines.* New York: Odyssey, 1999. **This book provides information on the history, customs, and people of the Philippines.**

FURTHER READING & WEBSITES

NONFICTION

Brittan, Dolly. *The People of the Philippines.* New York: PowerKids Press, 1997. **This book discusses the culture, religion, and beliefs of the people of the Philippines. It also examines the landscape of the country.**

Gonzales, Joaquin L. *The Philippines.* Milwaukee: Gareth Stevens Publishing, 2001. **This book explores the mix of native identities and foreign influences that shape the Philippines.**

Mendoza, Lunita. *Philippines.* Milwaukee: Gareth Stevens Publishing, 1999. **This book discusses the ways in which Filipino celebrations such as Ati-Atihan, Moriones, and Christmas reflect the culture of the Philippines.**

Nickels, Greg. *Philippines: The Culture.* New York: Crabtree Publishing Company, 2002. **Learn more about the people, weather, geography, and economy of the Philippines.**

Noriega, Violeta A. *Philippine Recipes Made Easy.* Kirkland, WA: Paperworks,

1993. **This cookbook is full of tasty and fun-to-make Filipino recipes.**

Oleksy, Walter G. *The Philippines.* New York: Children's Press, 2000. **This book explores the plants, animals, culture, sports, and arts of the Philippines.**

Sullivan, Margaret W. *The Philippines: Pacific Crossroads.* Parsippany, NJ: Dillon Press, 1998. **This book examines the history, culture, family life, and folklore of the Philippines, as well as Filipinos who have emigrated from the Philippines to the United States.**

Tope, Lily Rose R., and Detch P. Nonan–Mercado. *Philippines.* New York: Benchmark Books/Marshall Cavendish, 2002. **The authors provide an illustrated overview of the Philippines and its people.**

FICTION

Arcellana, Francisco. *The Mats.* Brooklyn: Kane/Miller Book Publishers, 1999. **In this story, a Filipino father returns from a** business trip with personalized sleeping mats for his family. Three of the mats have special significance.

Brainard, Cecilia Manguerra. *Growing Up Filipino: Stories for Young Adults.* Santa Monica, CA: Palh, 2003. **These short stories provide an in-depth look at what it means to be young and Filipino. Each story includes an introductory paragraph that explains some element of Filipino history or culture.**

de la Paz, Myrna J. *Abadeha: The Philippine Cinderella.* Auburn, CA: Shen's Books, 2001. **This book is a Filipino version of the classic fairy tale.**

Gilles, Almira Astudillo. *Willie Wins.* New York: Lee & Low Books, 2001. **This picture book gives readers a glimpse into Filipino culture through the story of a boy and his father.**

Guillermo, Artemio R. *Tales from the 7,000 Isles: Popular Philippine Folktales.* Mill Valley, CA: Vision Books International, 1996. **This book is a collection of Filipino folktales.**

Romulo, Liana. *Filipino Children's Favorite Stories.* North Clarendon, VT: Periplus Editions, 2000. **This book is**
a fun compilation of children's stories from the Philippines.

WEBSITES

FILIPINO AMERICAN NATIONAL HISTORICAL SOCIETY
http://www.fanhs-national.org
This website collects and shares information on the history and culture of Filipino immigrants to the United States.

INAMERICABOOKS.COM
http://www.inamericabooks.com
Visit www.inamericabooks.com, the online home of the In America series, to get linked to all sorts of useful information. You'll find historical and cultural websites related to individual groups as well as general information on genealogy, creating your own family tree, and the history of immigration in America.

THINGS ASIAN: EXPLORE THE CULTURES OF ASIA
http://www.thingsasian.com
This site offers stories, photos, travel information, and more about Asian countries, including the Philippines.

INDEX

National Women's Political Caucus, 60
Natividad, Irene, 60
New People's Army, 46
newspapers and magazines: *Filipino Students Magazine*, 25; *Republic*, 35
North America, history, 4

pensionados (scholarship students), 25
Philippines: ancient, 6–10; boundaries, location, and size, 6; Luzon (island), 6, 8, 10, 11, 26, 37; Magellan's voyage, 10–13; revolution, 19–21; Spanish rule, 13–16, 17, 18; U.S. territory, 20, 21–23, 47
Phillips, Lou Diamond, 60
population growth (Philippines), 46
poverty (Philippines), 46
presidents, U.S.: Johnson, Lyndon B., 44; Roosevelt, Franklin D., 37; Truman, Harry S., 41, 44

Quezon, Manuel, 60–61

race riots, 28
recipe, 51
religion: Buddhism, 15; Christianity, 11, 12, 13, 15; Hindu, 9; Islam, 10, 14, 15; Roman Catholicism, 15, 48, 52
Rescission Act, 42

Sakadas (contract workers), 5, 24, 25, 26, 30, 59
Salonga, Lea, 61
social or educational clubs, 34–35
stoop labor, 26–27
strikes, labor, 28, 29, 30, 60
students (self-supporting), 33–35. *See also* Blanco, Pedro M.

Tagalog. *See* language
Tydings–McDuffie Act, 22, 61

United States: Citizenship Retention and Re-acquisition Act of 2003, 44; discrimination against Filipinos, 5, 22, 27, 28, 31–32, 34, 42, 48; Filipino influence on, 5, 47, 49; Filipino Naturalization Act, 41–42; Filipino population in, 5, 32–33, 43; Great Depression, 29; Jones Act, 61; military, 36; Rescission Act, 42; Selective Service Act, 37, 38; Tydings–McDuffie Act, 22, 61; War Brides Act, 42, 44

Vergara–Paras, Lalaine, 61
veterans, 42
Villalobos, Ruy Lopez de, 13

War Brides Act, 42
war effort, contributions to, 40. *See also* military service, U.S.
wars and conflicts: Spanish–American War, 19; U.S. Revolutionary War, 4; World War II, 36–40, 41, 42, 44
wealth, unequal distribution of (Philippines), 46
World War II. *See* wars and conflicts

ACKNOWLEDGMENTS: THE PHOTOGRAPHS IN THIS BOOK ARE REPRODUCED WITH THE PERMISSION OF: Digital Vision Royalty Free, pp. 1, 3, 24; © Todd Strand/Independent Picture Service, p. 6; © Michael Rougier/Time Life Pictures/Getty Images, pp. 7, 29; © Mark Downey, pp. 8, 12, 41, 44, 49, 50; Library of Congress, pp. 10 (LC–USZ62–30424), 18 (LC–USZC4–4132), 20 (LC–USZC4–5958), 39 (LC–USZ62–80688); © Brown Brothers, pp. 11, 21; © CORBIS, p. 27; Shades of L.A. Archives/Los Angeles Public Library, pp. 31, 38, 40, 43; Minnesota Historical Society, p. 34; Martin Luther King Library, p. 45; © Douglas Peebles/CORBIS, p. 52; © Kathleen Voege/Getty Images, pp. 53, 54; © Terry Lilly/Zuma Press, p. 56; © CORBIS SYGMA, p. 57 (left); © Laura Farr/Zuma Press, p. 57 (right); © Zack Seckler/CORBIS, p. 58; © Christopher Felver/CORBIS, p. 59; © Lisa O'Connor/Zuma Press, p. 60 (top); © Bettmann/CORBIS, p. 60 (bottom); © Jamie Painter Young/CORBIS, p. 61 (left); © Paul Mounce/CORBIS, p. 61 (right); Maps by Bill Hauser, pp. 14, 32.

Cover photography by Sussman Studio, Minnesota Historical Society (top); © Todd Strand/Independent Picture Service (bottom); Digital Vision Royalty Free (title, back cover).